My Soul Doth Magnify the Lord

Inspirational poems and
devotions, salted with gems from
God's Holy Word

MARY WISHAM
FENSTERMACHER

WestBow
PRESS
A DIVISION OF THOMAS NELSON

ISBN: 978-1-4497-7422-6 (sc)
ISBN: 978-1-4497-7424-0 (hc)
ISBN: 978-1-4497-7423-3 (e)

Library of Congress Control Number: 2012922039

WestBow Press books may be ordered through booksellers or by contacting:

WestBow Press
A Division of Thomas Nelson
1663 Liberty Drive
Bloomington, IN 47403
www.westbowpress.com
1-(866) 928-1240

WestBow Press rev. date: 12/3/2012

In Loving Memory of...

Mildred MacPherson Wisham
(1920 - 1983)

...physical education teacher, physical therapist serving in WWII and the Korean Conflict, civics/ government teacher, recipient of the Classroom Teacher's Freedom Foundation Award Medal (Valley Forge, PA), and Sunday School teacher ~ my Mother.

In Heartfelt Love and Appreciation to...

Charles David Wisham

...telephone lineman and installer, airplane mechanic during WWII, Boy Scout leader, church trustee and deacon, faithful family man and provider, and generous supporter of my many writing projects ~ my Father.

With Love and Gratitude to...

Todd Edward Fenstermacher

...factory worker, insurance salesman, tax preparer, financial planner, doting father of our five children, and a caring helper during my various illnesses ~ my Husband.

I thank my God upon every remembrance of you.

~Philippians 1:3

Contents

God's Majestic Creation

Through the Seasons

Seaside Adventures

Christmas Tidings

Children's Corner ~ A Precious Parcel of Poems (for and about children)

Reflections

Luke 1:46-55

And Mary said, My soul doth magnify the Lord, And my spirit hath rejoiced in God my Savior. For He hath regarded the low estate of His handmaiden: for, behold, from henceforth all generations shall call me blessed.

For He that is mighty hath done to me great things; and Holy is His name. And His mercy is on them that fear Him from generation to generation. He hath shewed strength with His arm; He hath scattered the proud in the imagination of their hearts. He hath put down the mighty from their seats, and exalted them of low degree.

He hath filled the hungry with good things; and the rich He hath sent empty away. He hath holpen His servant Israel, in remembrance of His mercy; as He spake to our fathers, to Abraham, and to his seed forever.

Introduction

Over two millennia ago, a young mother-to-be exclaimed the words found in Luke 1:46-55, and these words would reverberate through the centuries as a timeless testimony to God's might and power. How blessed we are to have this same loving, caring, and unchanging Lord to guide us hundreds of years after Mary's baby was born. How blessed we are to know the ending of the story that began in the first chapter of Luke. How blessed we are to have the completed revelation of scriptures in our hands to read, digest, meditate on, and magnify on our earthly journey through life. How especially blessed we are to be in the position to receive Christ Jesus as our Savior, and to trust Him as our mediator before God the Father's throne.

Magnify means to make larger, amplify, or praise. Mary magnified the Lord's power, strength, and merciful character in her recitation to Elisabeth, her cousin, long ago. It is with this same admiration and desire to glorify God that these poems have been written and scriptures have been compiled. It is my heartfelt prayer, that each reader will come to see Christ magnified through the language of poetic verse, which has been initially inspired by God's Holy Word. The Bible truly is sharper than any two- edged sword, and is able to change any life, providing that that life is willing to accept the Heavenly Potter's hands.

My home is not of this world. Like many believers, I am a pilgrim wandering this land below, biding my time until I am whisked away to the heavenly mansions prepared above. In the meantime, God's gift of language has found sweet solace in my soul. Until the day my mansion is ready, I will continue to magnify my Lord in verse and song. In so doing, it is my prayer that many sisters and brothers in Christ, will be lifted up, encouraged, and confirmed through the sharing of these writings.

To God's Glory...
Mary Wisham Fenstermacher

Beginnings...

Genesis 1:1-5

In the beginning God created the heaven and the earth. And the earth was without form, and void; and darkness was upon the face of the deep. And the Spirit of God moved upon the face of the waters.

And God said, Let there be light: and there was light.

And God saw the light, that it was good: and God called the light Day, and the darkness He called Night. And the evening and the morning were the first day.

John 1:1-5

In the beginning was the Word, and the Word was with God, and the Word was God. The same was in the beginning with God.

All things were made by Him, and without Him was not anything made that was made.

In Him was life; and the life was the light of men.

And the light shineth in darkness; and the darkness comprehended it not.

Revelation 1:8

I am Alpha and Omega, the beginning and the ending, saith the Lord, which is, and was, and which is to come, the Almighty.

Blessings of Motherhood

~ Exodus 20:12 ~

Honour thy Father and thy Mother: that thy days may be
long upon the land which the Lord thy God giveth thee.

Jesus, Mary's Boy: God's Only Son

Luke 2:40-52

And the child grew, and waxed strong in spirit, filled with wisdom; and the grace of God was upon him.

Now his parents went to Jerusalem every year at the feast of the Passover.

And when he was twelve years old, they went up to Jerusalem after the custom of the feast.

And when they had fulfilled the days, as they returned, the child Jesus tarried behind in Jerusalem; and Joseph and his mother knew not of it.

But they, supposing him to have been in the company, went a day's journey; and they sought him among their kinsfolk and acquaintance.

And when they found him not, they turned back again to Jerusalem, seeking him.

And it came to pass, that after three days they found him in the temple, sitting in the midst of the doctors, both hearing them, and asking questions.

And all that heard him were astonished at his understanding and answers. And when they saw him, they were amazed: and his mother said unto him, Son, why hast thou thus dealt with us? Behold, thy father and I have sought thee sorrowing.

And he said unto them, "How is it that ye sought me? wist ye not that I must be about my Father's business?"

And they understood not the saying which he spake unto them.

And he went down with them, and came to Nazareth, and was subject unto them: but his mother kept all these sayings in her heart.

And Jesus increased in wisdom and stature, and in favour with God and man.

The Teachable Moment

Scripture: "Lo, children are an heritage of the Lord:
and the Fruit of the womb is His reward."

~ Psalm 127:3

So often, we mothers come to a point in our days, (weeks, lives) when we wonder what life is really about. A song writer in the 1960's wrote a piece entitled "Is That All There Is?" While I do not know the spiritual condition of that writer, the question asked is probably echoed time and again, by the saved and unsaved alike. Even Christians can get overburdened to the point that the "Joy of the Lord" gets lost in the shuffle of daily survival.

I can remember, quite vividly, a certain Saturday when I had a number of chores to get done within a short time period and the day was setting fast. Several loads of laundry were staring at me, and, of course, the sun was shining. I had to hang at least two loads outside. If I didn't, I would feel guilty for not being a good steward of our electricity. However, there were other chores rearing their ugly heads in the form of dirty breakfast and lunch dishes. In addition, I had important letters of correspondence to compose, address, and mail before the post office closed.

Now you may say, "No problem. Just set up a time schedule and dig in." Well, if you said that, your children must have left the nest already. At that time, I still had little ones underfoot and no amount of planning could guarantee a mission completed by the end of any day. "So what happened?" you ask.

The letters were written and sealed, but numerous interruptions, like "Mommy, I need a drink; Mommy, please tie my shoe; Mommy, I skinned my knee, I need a Band-Aid," peppered my afternoon workout. The post office closed without my visit.

As for the laundry, that did get done. Yes, sheets and permanent press got the royal treatment in God's great outdoors! Dinner was a virtual feast with vegetables from our very own garden. However, meal time didn't arrive until 7:30 p.m. Who can promise a 5:00 p.m. dinner for a family of seven every day?

In the midst of the sheer frustration of trying to get more done in a single day than humanly possible, an additional tugging was beginning to grab hold of my heart and mind. I was losing track of the real purpose of life in Christ. I had been letting things get in the way of God's joy and plans for me. The Lord's still, small voice chastised my self-imposed blindness and opened my eyes to a greater awareness of what really is important.

The result of this "teachable moment" is the poem "A Mother's Prayer."

A Mother's Prayer

Dearest Lord, there are quite a few days
When it shames my soul to have to say
That my human heart is in despair,
Crying out boldly a petitioner's prayer.

Help me, Dear Father, I'm bogged down with chores.
My duties each day keep me inside these doors.
Isn't there more to a mother's routine,
Than cleaning and cooking and babies to wean?

I'm swamped amid a mountain of clothing
Needing repair and wash machine loading.
In the kitchen, a stack of soiled plates
From breakfast, lunch, and snack time awaits.

My little ones playing outside send a call.
They need Mommy's help to fetch them their ball
That has rolled all the way across the wide street.
Then they beg me to get them something to eat.

Bureau drawers need straightening, closets, too.
Some days my work load seems so far from through.
Meals need preparation, bath time draws near.
The state of the household seems dull and drear.

But then, Dear Lord, your Holy Spirit soars
Within my heart, in the midst of my chores.
You bring to my mind a sweet special thing
That causes the gates of Heaven to ring.

My thoughts flood back with a most certain joy,
As echoes the prayer of my dear little boy.
With words of trust on his young childish lips,
His confession he makes, and Heaven he grips.

Another picture, as precious and sweet,
Is the little girl, who sits at my feet.
Mommy, I want to get saved, now, today.
Into my heart, I want Jesus to stay.

Suddenly now, on gossamer wings,
Life's burdens take flight; my happy heart sings.
Thank you Creator, Savior, and Lord,
For granting me blessings that gold can't afford.

This Mother's received a gift far out-priced.
God's given my little ones new life in Christ.
Never again will I cry nor complain,
But ponder with joy, salvation's great gain!

Thought: May we always be in remembrance that the greatest commission of motherhood is to teach, nurture, and train our little ones in the admonition of the Lord. (Ephesians 6:4 ~ And, ye fathers, [mothers] provoke not your children to wrath: but bring them up in the nurture and admonition of the Lord.) If we but carry out this command, our heavenly rewards will far exceed the number of dishes and clothes we have washed.

Prayer: Thank you, Lord, for the young ones that you have trustingly placed into our humble care. Grant us the wisdom and understanding that we need to nurture them through your Word, that one day, they too may take their place in Heaven's chorus, worshipping the Lamb as full citizens of thy kingdom. Thank you for bestowing such an awesome task, yet rewarding blessing among the duties of motherhood.

Titus 2:1-5

But speak thou the things which become sound doctrine:

That the aged men be sober, grave, temperate,
sound in faith, in charity, in patience.

The aged women likewise, that they be in behavior as becometh holiness,
not false accusers, not given to much wine; teachers of good things;

That they may teach the young women to be sober,
to love their husbands, to love their children,

To be discreet, chaste, keepers at home, good, obedient to their
own husbands, that the word of God be not blasphemed.

Mother

Someone very special
Has a place within my heart.
She lived this earth in beauty
'til that day she did depart.

She taught me all the normal things
A daughter needs to know—
Like cooking, cleaning, keeping house,
And learning how to sew.

But most of all she taught me
How a Christian ought to live.
She shared the joy of Jesus
So to others I might give.

She showed me through her actions
That Church I should attend.
As our family went to worship God—
Our broken hearts could mend.

Hard work and time, she sacrificed,
So I could go to Christian school;
Always teaching me and others
About God's Golden Rule.

Her life was spent for others—
Her family first, then friends.
Her care and loving kindness
Knew no boundaries or ends.

Her birthday soon will be here,
But no candles will be lit;
For she is up in Heaven—
In Christ's presence she does sit.

I praise God for my Mother
Who loved and trained me in His Word.
Now, I can share Christ's Gospel—
The Sweetest Story Ever Heard!

Proverbs 31: 10-31

~ A Virtuous Woman ~

Who can find a virtuous woman? For her price is far above rubies.

The heart of her husband doth safely trust in her, so that he shall have no need of spoil.

She will do him good and not evil all the days of her life.

She seeketh wool, and flax, and worketh willingly with her hands.

She is like the merchants' ships; she bringeth her food from afar.

She riseth also while it is yet night, and giveth meat to her household, and a portion to her maidens.

She girdeth her loins with strength, and strengtheneth her arms.

She perceiveth that her merchandise is good: her candle goeth not out by night.

She layeth her hands to the spindle, and her hands hold the distaff.

She stretcheth out her hand to the poor; yea, she reacheth forth her hands to the needy.

She is not afraid of the snow for her household: for all her household are clothed with scarlet.

She maketh herself coverings of tapestry; her clothing is silk and purple.

Her husband is known in the gates, when he sitteth among the elders of the land.

She maketh fine linen, and selleth it; and delivereth girdles unto the merchant.

Strength and honour are her clothing; and she shall rejoice in time to come.

She openeth her mouth with wisdom; and in her tongue is the law of kindness.

She looketh well to the ways of her household, and eateth not the bread of idleness.

Her children rise up, and call her blessed; her husband also, and he praiseth her.

Many daughters have done virtuously, but thou excellest them all.

Favour is deceitful, and beauty is vain: but a woman that feareth the Lord, she shall be praised.

Give her of the fruit of her hands; and let her own works praise her in the gates.

The Beatitudes

~ Matthew 5:2-12 ~

And He opened his mouth, and taught them, saying

Blessed are the poor in spirit: for their's is the kingdom of heaven.

Blessed are they that mourn: for they shall be comforted.

Blessed are the meek: for they shall inherit the earth.

Blessed are they which do hunger and thirst after righteousness: for they shall be filled.

Blessed are the merciful: for they shall obtain mercy.

Blessed are the pure in heart: for they shall see God.

Blessed are the peacemakers: for they shall be called the children of God.

Blessed are they which are persecuted for righteousness' sake: for their's is the kingdom of heaven.

Blessed are ye, when men shall revile you, and persecute you, and shall say all manner of evil against you falsely, for my sake.

Rejoice, and be exceeding glad: for great is your reward in heaven: for so persecuted they the prophets which were before you.

~A Special Note ~

If you are a Mother, you no doubt have experienced one or more
of the circumstances described in the following poems.

Read, weep, giggle…enjoy!!!

If you aren't a mother, stand in awe of Motherhood and the many
duties mothers are called upon to perform EVERY DAY…

God's grace is sufficient!

Mommy, I Am Hungry

Mommy, I am HUNGRY!
Mommy, I am STARVED!
Mommy, my poor tummy
Is G-R-O-W-L-I-N-G very hard!

Please, hurry quick and feed me
Some yummy food and drink.
My tummy is s-o-o-o HUNGRY
It might eat me up, I think!

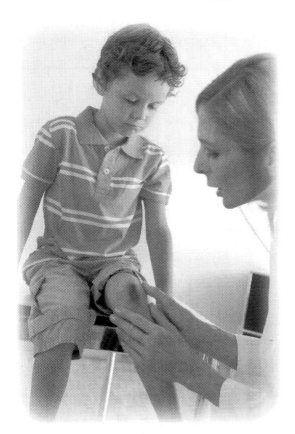

Mommy, I Fell Down

Mommy, Mommy, I fell down
I think I may have broke my crown!
Mommy, my poor knee is hurt.
It's all messed up with stones and dirt.
Mommy, mommy, help me please;
Put some Band-Aids on my knees.
You can kiss away my tears
And sing a song to chase my fears.

Mommy, Look At Me!!!

Mommy, come and look at me!
I can surely climb a tree.
I can ride my three wheel bike
And walk with Daddy on a hike.

Mommy, I can do so much—
Rake the yard or play with trucks.
I can hit the ball real far
Or help my daddy wash his car.

I am growing up, you know
And soon to school, I'll gladly go.
Mommy, Mommy, look at me.
Soon no more will I be three!

Mommy, Can I Help?

Mommy, can I help you, please?
I promise I'll work carefully.
Can I help you bake a cake
And watch you as the meal you make?

Maybe I could crack the eggs—
If only taller were my legs.
I wish that I could reach the sink,
Then I could get my own cold drink.

Mommy, when will I be able
To help you daily set the table?
When I'm five or maybe six,
Can I perhaps the dinner fix?

I really hope that someday soon—
Maybe April, May or June,
I will be good help for you;
I'm hoping that the months are few!

The Party

Mommy, see my party dress!
I'll be real careful not to mess.
Black shiny shoes upon my feet,
Make my outfit quite complete.

Now, I'm ready for the party.
I must hurry so I'm not tardy.
My friend is turning seven today
And we have plans for games to play.

Count the buttons in the jar, and
Throw a ball to see how far
It rolls across the big backyard,
To win the champion ribbon card.

I wonder how the cake will be.
I hope it's nice and chocolate—y;
And the ice cream cold and sweet
Will make a tasty noontime treat.

The party gift is wrapped so neat.
Now it's time for me to greet
My birthday friend across the way—
It's going to be a super day!

Help!

Help! Help! My tongue is stuck.

I was trying to drink from my

little blue cup.

That mean old ice cube

jumped right up;

and to the end of my tongue—

it stuck!

Words of Faith & Hope

~Matthew 17:20~

And Jesus said unto them… for verily I say unto you, If ye have faith as a grain of mustard seed, ye shall say unto this mountain, Remove hence to yonder place; and it shall remove; and nothing shall be impossible unto you.

✛

The Mustard Seed

I was first introduced to the mustard seed when one of my elementary school teachers gave me a tiny mustard seed. It was protected inside a small glass ball and clasped to a shiny chain bracelet. It is amazing to learn that this tiny seed, when watered and properly nourished will grow into a three foot stalk bearing many leaves measuring two feet long.

Jesus said if we have even the slightest faith, the size of a grain of mustard seed, we could move mountains. As a child, I felt that that was a difficult statement to comprehend. It was hard for me to visualize how I could climb a tall mountain, let alone move one!

As an adult I have come to understand Christ's teachings a little better. Life is filled with mountains of human disappointments, struggles, pain, and sorrow. Jesus experienced these human frailties as He met them on a daily basis. He was God--living on earth. How painful it must have been for Him to dwell among sinful men and women. How saddened He must have been each time a lost soul rejected Him, the God of creation.

The good news is that Christ died for all of the perpetrators of sin's evil ways. Jesus Christ died on the cross of Calvary. Therein lies our hope! Hope for mankind began with the victory Christ secured over sin on that day He shed His life's blood for all.

This brings us back to the mustard seed. All you need is the faith of a mustard seed, or even the faith of a small child, and God will help you overcome your mountains. Faith in His saving grace will also grant you a home in His heavenly kingdom.

✝

~ *Romans 8:26-28* ~

Likewise the Spirit also helpeth our infirmities: for we know not what we should pray for as we ought: but the Spirit itself maketh intercession for us with groanings which cannot be uttered.

And He that searcheth the hearts knoweth what is the mind of the Spirit, because He maketh intercession for the saints according to the will of God.

And we know that all things work together for good to them that love God, to them who are the called according to His purpose.

✝

Lo, I Am with You Always

Scripture: All things work together for good, to them that love God, to them that are the called according to His purpose.

~Romans 8:28

It was an ordinary day. Breakfast was finished and the children had begun their school lessons. I was tidying the kitchen when the phone rang. My mind was not prepared to receive the news at the other end of the line. A friend sadly informed me that a mutual friend had just lost her four month old fetus. The baby's heart was no longer beating when given a routine check at the doctor's office.

I was stunned. My mother's heart wept and tears filled my eyes. What could I do? What should I say? Would a phone call help? Probably not. I am too prone to crying when emotional. That certainly wouldn't help my grieving friend. I purposed to quiet my sympathizing heart and listen to the Lord's still small voice. Waiting on Him is a privilege I have learned to savor. Waiting is an exercise in faith; faith in God's promise that He is always with us. I have also found that there is a true blessing at the end of the wait.

This particular wait took only two days. I turned to God's gift of language to help comfort my sister in Christ and began writing a card and letter of encouragement. As I wrote, an additional urging tugged at my heart. Bible verses, thoughts, words, came tumbling down from Heaven's word bank. The poem, Hold Fast, was penned in less than an hour. I typed it, printed it out, and sent it off with a prayer that its message of comfort would lighten the load of this dear, sorrowing friend and her family. Little did I know that this very same poem would also become a special blessing to my father-in-law who was struggling with cancer.

The Bible says God uses the foolish things of life to confound man. Some folks may find poetry to be an unnecessary frivolity. I would mention,

✝

however, that there is a lot of poetry in God's Word. Sharing scripture through poetry, then, seems to be a natural way to benefit from God's gift of language. Poetry based on scripture is a tangible way to help us remember God's promises.

Thought: Has not God said, Heaven and Earth shall pass away, but my Words shall never pass away? Since this is so, how much more assured we can be of God's everlasting presence among us. Let this fact be a reaffirmation that the Lord's promise Lo, I am with you alway is one we can cling to in whatever circumstance we find ourselves.

Prayer: Heavenly Father, grant us the grace to accept the things we cannot change and cling to the promise that you are with us always. Remind us that you are the master designer and that all things work together for good, even though our human heart and mind cannot comprehend your plan. Increase our faith, dear Lord, that we may live above our circumstances.

✟

~II Timothy 1:13, 14~

Hold fast the form of sound words, which thou hast heard
of me, in faith and love which is in Christ Jesus.

That good thing which was committed unto thee keep
by the Holy Ghost which dwelleth in us.

~ Thessalonians 5:21 ~

Prove all things; hold fast that which is good.

Hold Fast

We often do not understand
    Why things happen as they do.
Why pain and disappointments come
    And wrench our hearts clear through.

We cannot know the mind of God
    In every circumstance,
For He's the great Creator,
    He rules the world's expanse.

We do know that God's Love is deep
    He sacrificed His Son
To be our blessed Redeemer—
    Against the foe He has won.

"All things work together for good"
    In Romans this statement is clear.
Although it is sometimes hard to accept,
    God's way is the best and most dear.

Hold Fast to the Lord's sure promise—
    "Lo, I am with you alway".
Take heart that this trial which besets you,
    Will fade in God's grace as you pray.

✝

Joshua 1:8, 9

This book of the law shall not depart out of thy mouth, but thou shalt meditate therein day and night, that thou mayest observe to do according to all that is written therein: for then thou shalt make thy way prosperous, and then thou shalt have good success.

Have not I commanded thee?

Be strong and of good courage; be not afraid, neither be thou dismayed: for the Lord thy God is with thee withersoever thou goest.

Ephesians 6:10, 11

Finally, my brethren, be strong in the Lord, and in the power of his might.

Put on the whole armour of God, that ye may be able to stand against the wiles of the devil.

✝

Be Strong

"Dear Lord, this trial is way too hard,"
My fainting soul cried out.
Tears began to trickle down
My faith was far from stout.

I did not know which step to take
Or who to call for aid.
My quivering lips could only plead
To the One, Whom all things made.

Soon a voice, still, soft and small
Came whispering to my ear.
"Do not be discouraged child
Be strong and of good cheer.

Do not let your spirit fail—
My strength is all you need.
My grace is all sufficient;
To My Holy Word take heed.

Keep the faith within your heart
Don't let your hope be shaken;
Be strong of heart and courage,
On My yoke, your cares I've taken.

✝

Remember, I built mountain peaks
From bits of rock and sand.
I framed the world with clouds and stars
Placed there by My own hand."

So, when you find you're feeling low
Rest on the Savior's power.
His mighty strength can lift you up
Any time of day or hour.

✝

~ *John 14:6* ~

Jesus saith unto him,

I Am the way, the truth, and the life: no man
cometh unto the Father, but by me.

~*John 11:25-27*~

Jesus said unto her,

I Am the Resurrection and the Life: he that believeth
in me, though he were dead, yet shall he live:

And whosoever liveth and believeth in me
shall never die. Believest thou this?

She saith unto Him, Yea, Lord: I believe that thou art the
Christ, the Son of God, which should come into the world.

✞

Redeemer Mine

In Christ, the Rock, I take my stand;
He guides me with His outstretched hand.
No other one wields greater power;
His Wisdom leads me every hour.
He is the Way, the Truth, the Life.
His Grace and Mercy quench all strife.
His Grace and Mercy quench all strife.

His life He gave—a slaughtered lamb;
Now reigns in Heav'n, the Great I Am.
He is the resurrection gift;
Now unto Him, my praise I lift.
O Holy One, Redeemer mine,
Did bear my sins to make me Thine.
Did bear my sins to make me Thine.

Christ is the Door that guards the sheep;
He rules each day, my soul does keep.
He is the Light, the Living Bread;
The Church He bought and rules as Head.
I am the branch. Christ is the vine.
He dwells in me, yes, He is mine.
He dwells in me, yes, He is mine.

(These verses may be sung to the tune "The Solid Rock.")

✟

A House Not Made with Hands

*Scripture: For our light affliction, which is but for a moment,
worketh for us a far more exceeding and eternal weight of glory;*

*While we look not at the things which are seen, but at the
things which are not seen: for the things which are seen are
temporal; but the things which are not seen are eternal.*

*For we know that if our earthly house of this tabernacle were dissolved, we
have a building of God, an house not made with hands, eternal in the heavens.*

~II Corinthians 4:17, 18 and 5:1

Summer was coming to an end. Our eldest daughter would
soon be returning to college—a difficult season of good-byes,
especially for her younger siblings. (Parents are supposed to
take this separation in stride?!) In addition to losing a daughter
for another college semester, our family was experiencing some
other 'lows' in our day to day living. The "who can we rob to pay
Paul" syndrome was reaching an all-time high. That week was
not one of our mountain top experiences by a long shot.

I sat in our living room seeking some deeply sought after
serenity—the kind of solitude only a mother could cherish.
As I read my devotions, a Christian music tape was playing
softly in the background. I reveled in the quietness of the early
morning hour. With preschoolers in the house, it is difficult to
grab a sizeable block of peace and quiet. I had almost finished
my Bible reading when padding feet could be heard making
their way down the hardwood hallway. I mustered as much
patience as I could while my four year old tumbled into my
lap.

✛

As sweetly as possible, I indicated that Mommy needed just a few more minutes of quiet. To my surprise he co-operated and we snuggled together around the Bible. My mind returned once again to the earnest, prayerful pleas for God's help with our current financial concerns. My petition was interrupted when the little voice upon my knee wanted to know more about the tree in the song that was playing.

"Mommy, they nailed Jesus to that tree, didn't they?"

My attention was captured with the abruptness of an explosion. My youngest child, of his own free will, had begun a conversation, which minutes later, led to his new life in Christ!

Isn't it special how God can take our worries and concerns and turn them into memorable and heaven glorifying events in our life? It reminds me of the time Jesus turned the water into wine at the marriage feast in Cana. (John 2) Sometimes our priorities get terribly out of focus. Mary, the mother of Jesus, wanted to be of help to the wedding couple. They were beside themselves with worry because their wine supply had diminished. They were at their wits end. Mary knew Jesus could solve their problem and He did solve it quite miraculously. But I often wonder if Jesus would have much rather given them the water of life on that important day.

In my case, God performed a miracle as well as a sudden change of priorities. One minute I was pleading for directions and help to deal with life in the natural realm; and the next minute the Lord was drawing the attention of my whole being to that of the Spiritual realm. My prayer for temporal needs was turned into a prayer of salvation with and for my young son!

Life on earth will always be filled with one trial or another. Trials come and go; but God has not left us helpless. His Word says "But my God shall supply all your need according to His riches in glory by Christ Jesus." (Philippians 4:19) The most miraculous thing about that special summer morning was that a little boy accepted Christ as his Lord and Savior. No one will ever be able to take this decision from him. "And I give unto them eternal life; and they shall never perish, neither shall any man pluck them out of my hand." (John 10:28) Best of all, is the eternal home my son will have in Heaven one day. Yes, Heaven is Salvation's glorious gift!

Thought: Jesus said to His disciples in Mark 14:7, "Ye have the poor with you always, and whensoever ye will, ye may do them good: but me ye have not always." Why can't we learn more quickly from the scriptures that time spent with Jesus will always outweigh, overshadow, and be greater times of blessings, than the time we spend entangling ourselves in the affairs of the world? (see II Timothy 2:3,4)

Prayer: Dear Lord and Author of Salvation, we humbly admit that too often we struggle and entangle ourselves in the matters of human existence, so much so, that we forget about the gift that salvation brings. Thank you for carrying us over the rough spots in our life, and for giving us the hope and courage to press on. Thank you for brightening our valleys with glimpses of mountain tops from time to time. Keep us ever moving upward as we journey toward Heaven's eternal home.

✞

~ *Romans* 10:13 ~

For WHOSOEVER shall call upon the name of the Lord shall be saved.

~*Ephesians* 2:8~

For by grace are ye saved through faith; and that
not of yourselves: it is the gift of God:

✝

Salvation's Gift

Just when our hearts are trembling with doubt,
God sends us a joy to praise Him about.
Dark paths and valleys seem ever so low,
But tall mountain peaks make faces glow.

Thank you, Dear Lord, for Thy loving care;
When troubled souls are tossed in despair.
Thank you for lifting us out of the storm,
Surrounding our lives with your love so warm.

Lift our eyes in faith to Thy strong, kind face,
No matter how long or hard looms the race.
Praise evermore blessed Lord up on high,
For Salvation's great gift—the Sweet By and By !

✝

John 14:1-3

Let not your heart be troubled: ye believe in God,
believe also in me.
In my Father's house are many mansions:
if it were not so, I would have told you.
I go to prepare a place for you.
And if I go and prepare a place for you,
I will come again, and receive you unto myself;
that where I am, there ye may be also.

✝

Heaven

There is a land far brighter
Than the one we trod today.
There is a hope far grander
Than this world could e'er display.

There is a love far more complete
Than relations here below;
For the God of Grace in Heaven
Provides mansions where blessings flow.

There is no need for sunshine.
Christ's glory will light our days.
No tears will dampen our eyelids;
On scenes of paradise we'll gaze.

Grand golden streets of glory
Lead to God's majestic throne.
Praise God for salvation that grants us rest,
In Heaven's eternal home.

So, when dark days of earth are o'er
And we've seen the last setting sun.
Rejoice in the Lord of Heaven
As we meet face to face His Son!

✝

A Pilgrim's Prayer

When people all around me snap with bitterness and hate,

My fortitude starts weakening; I long for Heaven's gate.

I find that I am standing here ~ frustrated and alone.

I yearn for Christ's Great Wisdom; I yearn for Heaven's home.

I try Christ's Words to follow and turn the other cheek;

But every time I feel sin's slap, Christ's loving arms I seek.

To live God's way is difficult; the path is rough and steep.

As Pilgrims in the days of old, life's trials and pain I reap.

Dear Jesus, Lord and Savior, Your power and strength I need.

Protect me from sin's awful sway; my steps, I pray, you'll lead.

Direct my path in sovereignty; make known to me Thy Will.

Keep me strong, unfettered, as I struggle up each hill.

Surround me with Thy loving arms; uplift my fainting heart.

Encourage me along life's way--my shield from Satan's dart.

Dear Jesus, King of Glory, impart to me Thy Grace.

Keep me in Thy constant care 'til I meet You face to face.

Stressed Out

Scripture: These things have I spoken unto you, that in Me ye might have peace. In the world ye shall have tribulation: but be of good cheer; I have overcome the world.

~ John 16:33

I often wonder what people of long ago used as a buzz word for worry, anxiety, and tribulation. Stress is the word of our generation. Being "stressed out" seems to be a commonplace malady. Today there is such an emphasis on stress management. Businesses, schools, and hospitals provide classes for their employees to help them deal with the stressful circumstances in their lives. Television commercials cajole their viewers to break free from their troubles and fly to Bermuda, the Caribbean or Hawaii!

But what does the Bible say?

In the thirteenth through seventeenth chapters of John, Jesus shared important, final thoughts and concerns with His disciples in the Upper Room. He warned that they would be scattered, put out of the synagogues, would be killed—and by those who thought they were doing service to God. These would certainly be stressful times for Christ's followers. Jesus knew this and left them the hope, care, and guidance of the comforter. "And when he is come, he will reprove the world of sin, and of righteousness, and of judgment... (John 16:8)...he will guide you into all truth:...(John 16:13a)...and he will shew you things to come. (John 16:13c)

Our Creator truly is omniscient. He planned for our well-being even before we were born—before we ourselves knew our needs. He gave us His Word to read, study, and apply to our lives. When we become overburdened with stress, trials, and worries there is a place of quietness. How much closer to the heart of God can one be than to nourish one's heart and mind on the Bread of Life?

Prayer is also a helpful and comforting practice during the throes of affliction. Christ prayed for his disciples before He left for Glory and promised them the Spirit of Truth. This promise was not only for the disciples, but is one we may claim even today. John 17:20 says,

> "Neither pray I for these alone, but for them also which shall believe on me through their word…"

What a blessing to know that even at this very moment, Christ's prayers of intercession on our behalf can be heard before Heaven's throne.

Our human hearts may falter, our spirit my whither in the face of adversity, but we need not despair for Christ has overcome the world and has left the Comforter to guide our steps. Christ can be at your helm day to day, trial to trial, and minute to minute.

The big question is: Will you let Him?

✝

Thought: The captain of a ship has high powers of authority when out to sea. He is ultimately responsible for all navigating decisions which affect the lives of every crew member and passenger on board. He has the power to perform wedding ceremonies and burial services.

If our society can bestow such authority upon one human being, why should it be so difficult to let the Creator and Savior of the world sit at our helm?

Prayer: Precious Savior, help us to realize that you are all sufficient in our deepest trials. Too often, we look to books and people with important titles to help us solve our problems. Please bring to our remembrance the truths found in your Holy Word. Help us to claim your promises of hope and learn to fully trust, in faith believing, your power and worthiness to steer our helm.

✝

~ II Corinthians 12:9 ~

And he said unto me,

My grace is sufficient for thee: for my

strength is made perfect in weakness.

Most gladly therefore will I rather glory in my

infirmities, that the power of Christ may rest

upon me.

✝

The Helm

When stress and worry overwhelm
I sometimes fear I've lost the helm.
But Christ's the captain of my soul,
His guiding strength and love console.

His power overcomes my fears.
His healing hands remove all tears.
He's the One to whom I turn
When for peace and hope I yearn.

Don't let snares of sin prevail.
The Lord of Heaven cannot fail.
Christ's the One who answers prayers.
He's the Friend who always cares.

When stress and worry overwhelm,
Remember, Christ is at the helm!

✝

I John 4:7-11

Beloved, let us love one another: for love
is of God; and every one that loveth is
born of God, and knoweth God.

He that loveth not knoweth not
God; for God is Love.

In this was manifested the love of God toward
us, because that God sent his only begotten Son
into the world, that we might live through him.

Herein is love, not that we loved God,
but that he loved us, and sent his Son
to be the propitiation for our sins.

Beloved, if God so loved us, we
ought also to love one another.

✝

Three Words

There are three words we often use
That grant us hope and cheer.
They let a fellow Christian know
Their Savior's always near.

There are three words we often use
To comfort, calm, and share—
The peace and love of the Master,
When a heart-sick soul's in despair.

The words—Jesus Loves You—are music
To the sorrowing brother in pain.
They comfort the one who's lost a friend,
Or the child crying out in the rain.

Jesus Loves You, is a promise to all,
For the Bible says "God is Love".
Therefore, we know, saying "Jesus Loves You"
Will spread peace to our hearts like a dove.

✝

~Psalm 145:9-13~

The Lord is good to all: and his tender mercies are over all his works.

All thy works shall praise thee, O Lord; and thy saints shall bless thee.

They shall speak of the glory of thy kingdom, and talk of thy power;

To make known to the sons of men his mighty acts,
and the glorious majesty of his kingdom.

Thy kingdom is an everlasting kingdom, and thy
dominion endureth throughout all generations.

~Jude 1:25~

To the only wise God our Saviour, be glory and majesty,
dominion and power, both now and ever. Amen.

God's Majestic Creation

~ Psalm 148: 1-5 ~

Praise ye the Lord. Praise ye the Lord from the
heavens: praise him in the heights.

Praise ye him, all his angels: praise ye him, all his hosts.

Praise ye him, sun and moon: praise him, all ye stars of light.

Praise him, ye heavens of heavens, and ye
waters that be above the heavens.

Let them praise the name of the Lord: for he
commanded, and they were created.

~Psalm 19:1~

The heaven's declare the glory of God; and the
firmament sheweth his handiwork.

~Genesis 1:31~

And God saw everything that He had made, and behold, it was
very good. And the evening and the morning were the sixth day.

~Revelation 5:11, 12~

And I beheld, and I heard the voice of many angels round about the
throne and the beasts and the elders: and the number of them was
ten thousand times ten thousand, and thousands and thousands;

Saying with a loud voice, Worthy is the Lamb that was
slain to receive power, and riches, and wisdom, and
strength, and honour, and glory, and blessing.

God's Wonderful World

Poems found in this section were inspired by simply observing God's creation. Some poems were written as I gazed out our living room window. There are tree covered foothills centered in this oversized picture window that provide natural beauty for the onlooker, whether it be summer, spring, winter, or fall. Through this window, I could see the sun glistening on the treetops and watch the clouds shading the valley below. It was then that *Evening at Sunset* was penned.

What happened outside our kitchen window was also a source of excitement and cheerful animation. Squirrels, cardinals, goldfinch, mourning doves and other colorful birds were constantly battling for their share of birdseeds in our front yard feeder. *Two Blue Jays* and *God's Creatures* are results of these engaging moments. Watching God's handiwork is an enjoyable and wonderful blessing He has graciously given to us.

It is important for us to understand that God did not stop on the seventh day of His creative acts. There is something more important, something beyond watching the squirrels play, birds feasting on birdseeds, and colorful leaves decorating autumn trees. The Lord was not finished. God knew that humankind, even though he had already been so blessed, would not "make the cut". He knew human weaknesses would prevent mankind from reaching the goal, God's Kingdom, without providential help.

God made a beautiful world of rocks, trees, rivers, mountains, and oceans for mankind to explore and enjoy. Unfortunately, sin entered the world when the forbidden fruit was eaten. The Creator did not give up on His creation, however. He made a plan—a plan so loving, so compassionate, and so sacrificial, it is difficult to comprehend. He set on course the plan of salvation when His own Son, the Lamb of God, was slain to set His world free and save humankind from their sinful ways.

Yes, there is a place Beyond Creation…

Beyond Creation

The Psalmist, long ago, exclaimed:
The Heavens declare God's glory.
The Lord Himself hung the moon and stars
So began His handiwork story.

The waters, He parted from the land,
The land away from the sky.
Daylight and nighttime made one full day;
'Tis "good" the Creator did cry!

Soon there appeared trees, flowers, and plants
Made in God's omnipotent act.
Fowl of the air and creatures on land
Are results of this marvelous fact.

The Lord knew well he was not done,
And created a man in His image.
Adam the first man made by God
Would begin a most proud royal lineage.

Time went on. God's work was just fine;
But man ignored his Creator.
He worshipped instead the things that were made
Forgetting the omniscient Savior.

God was much grieved and felt sorrow,
For the plan of salvation brought pain.
His Son, the "I Am" of all ages,
Must suffer sin's price and be slain.

Worthy is He that has bought us
With His shed blood on Calvary's tree.
Worthy is He that has saved us
From a sin scarred world—now we're free!

Yes, Christ, the Word spoke creation,
But the story goes on past Day Seven.
God let this all happen with purpose—
That His children might join Him in Heaven.

~Psalm 92: 1-5~

It is a good thing to give thanks unto the Lord, and
to sing praises unto thy name. O most High;

To shew forth thy lovingkindness in the morning,
and thy faithfulness every night,

Upon an instrument of ten strings, and upon the
psaltery; upon the harp with a solemn sound.

For thou, Lord, hast made me glad through thy work:
I will triumph in the works of thy hands.

O Lord, how great are thy works! And thy thoughts are very deep.

I Thank Him

I thank God for the mountains.
I thank Him for the skies.
I thank Him for His mighty acts
That all around me lies.
I thank God for His kindness.
I thank Him for His love.
I thank Him for His Only Son
That came from heaven above.

I thank God for His goodness.
I thank Him every day.
I thank Him for His faithfulness
That keeps me lest I stray.
I thank God for His patience.
Each day I praise Him more.
I thank Him for His Holy Word
That forever will endure.

I thank God for the flowers.
I thank Him for each tree.
I thank Him for His loving Son
That died to make me free.
I thank God for His power
And great, strong, loving care.
I thank Him for the day
That I will meet Him in the air!

~Psalm 30:4, 5~

Sing unto the Lord, O ye saints of his,

and give thanks at the remembrance of his holiness.

For his anger endureth but a moment;

in his favour is life: weeping may endure for

a night, but joy cometh in the morning.

Birth of a Poem

I awoke with a start this morning
Hearing twitters of local birds.
Pictures rushed into my mind
As I searched for the perfect words.

O'er and o'er I repeated them—
So cozy in my bed,
Knowing that it would be a risk
To trust them to my head.

I struggled from my warm, repose
Groping for paper and pen,
And wrote the words to the poem
About dawning of morn near the glen.

~Lamentations 3:22, 23~

It is of the Lord's mercies that we are not consumed,
because His compassions fail not.

They are new every morning: great is thy faithfulness.

Morning's Dawn

As nighttime's darkness lifts its shade,
The morning sun begins to invade
Nooks and valleys of rolling hills.
Waking birds unmask hidden bills.

The stillness of the long dark night
Is broken by the day's new light.
Sounds of whippoorwill and waking wrens
Are heard along the distant glens.

Dewdrops glisten on garden plants;
The day begins for busy ants.
Chipmunks scamper across the lawn,
Breathing the freshness of morning's dawn.

Gentle winds whisper through towering trees;
Birds soar high on a lofty breeze.
Fluffly white clouds float through a blue sky;
The coming of day has again drawn nigh!

~Genesis 1:19-21~

And the evening and the morning
were the fourth day.

And God said, Let the waters bring forth
abundantly the moving creature that
hath life, and fowl that may fly above the
earth in the open firmament of heaven.

And God created great whales, and every
living creature that moveth, which the
waters brought forth abundantly, after
their kind, and every winged fowl after
his kind: and God saw that it was good.

God's Creatures

The house finch at the feeder,
Doves resting on the ground,
The robin singing sweetly,
As cardinals fly around—

All are God's own creatures,
He watches o'er each one.
He loves and cares for me, too.
He saved me through His Son!

~Matthew 6:26, 28, 29~

Behold the fowls of the air: for they sow not, neither do they reap, nor gather into barns; yet your heavenly Father feedeth them. Are ye not much better than they?

And why take ye thought for raiment? Consider the lilies of the field, how they grow; they toil not, neither do they spin:

And yet I say unto you, That even Solomon in all his glory was not arrayed like one of these.

Two Blue Jays

Two blue jays out my window
Underneath the birch tree sit.
They peck through snow for birdseeds
As the wind makes birch bark flit.

Blue skies are filled with sunshine
But the wind is harsh and cold.
Still, the feathered friends keep pecking—
Their breakfast, brave and bold.

I wondered as I watched them
How these small and lovely birds
Could survive in such fierce weather,
'Twas a marvel beyond words!

God sent a quick reminder,
"I made these creatures, small.
I protect them like the lilies.
I guard them winter through fall."

How great is God our Creator
Who cares for the greatest and least.
He guides His creation safely
From each person to smallest beast.

~Psalm 50:1~

The mighty God, even the Lord, hath spoken, and called the earth from the rising of the sun unto the going down thereof.

~Ecclesiastes 1:5~

The sun also riseth, and the sun goeth down, And hasteth to his place where he arose.

Evening at Sunset

There is a sweet calm stillness
    That settles in my heart;
It comes as day is waning
    And the sun starts to depart.

Sun rays rest on distant trees
    Along the mountain trail.
Shadows cast by passing clouds,
    Dance upon the vale.

Songs of birds and cricket sounds
    Sing peace into the air;
A gentle breeze of springtime warmth
    Comforts every care.

Sunset is that time of day
    When, almost, time stands still—
Until the round, red glowing ball
    Dips beyond the hill.

~Genesis 8:22~

While the earth remaineth,
seedtime and harvest, and cold and heat,
and summer and winter, and day and night shall not cease.

Through the Seasons

~Ecclesiastes 3:1~

To every thing there is a season, and a time to
every purpose under the heaven:

~Genesis 1:14~

And God said, Let there be lights in the firmament of the heaven to divide the day from the night; and let them be for signs, and for seasons, and for days, and years;

A Time of Thanks

While the official Thanksgiving Day in America is celebrated on the fourth Thursday of November, many people believe that every day should be a day of thanksgiving to the Lord for His mercies. I am of that belief.

God makes the world turn. He changes the seasons. He waters the earth with snow and rain from the firmament above. He warms His creation with rays from the glowing sun that He made with His own hands. The Bible tells us if we do not praise our Creator, the rocks will surely cry out!

Who, but God, can paint the autumn leaves and adorn the apple trees with fruit of red, green, and gold? Who but the Creator of seasons can produce billions of snowflakes, each one unique from the others? Who can take the cold frozen world of winter and revive it through the rebirth of springtime freshness, beauty, and warmth? Who, but Almighty God, loved His handiwork so much that He would sacrifice His only begotten Son to save humankind from their sinful ways?

Yes, the God of autumn, winter, spring, and summer is forever overseeing His creation. He is in control. He is always there. All thanks be to God!

He will not suffer thy foot to be moved: He that
keepeth thee will not slumber. ~Psalm 121:3

~ Psalm 65:13 ~

The pastures are clothed with flocks; the valleys also are covered over with corn; they shout for joy, they also sing.

~ Daniel 2:20-21a~

Daniel answered and said, Blessed be the name of God for ever and ever: for wisdom and might are His: And He changeth the times and the seasons:

Autumn Song

Skies are painted with patches
of fluffy white on blue.
Maples and Oaks are glowing
with a red and golden hue.

Mountain streams are gurgling
as they meander from their source.
Hillsides are speckled with grazing cattle;
yonder echoes a neighing horse.

The air is crisp; the wind foretells
an approaching change of weather.
The sunset darkens the evening sky;
a chickadee ruffles its feather.

Summer days of sun and pleasure
have escaped us once again;
But the glorious song of autumn
is ready to begin!

~Matthew 9:37-38~

Then saith He unto His disciples, The harvest truly is plenteous, but the labourers are few; Pray ye therefore the Lord of the harvest, that He will send forth labourers unto His harvest.

Thanksgiving Time

Once again the table's spread
With bounties from the Lord;
And everyone is seated
Around the family board.

The large, brown, juicy turkey
Is ready for the carving;
While hungry, wide-eyed children
Lick their lips as if they're starving.

Thanksgiving is that special day
When loved ones join together,
To praise the Lord of harvest,
Who reigns on high forever.

Thank you, Heavenly Father,
For blessings set before us.
Thank you, for Thy love and care;
For all things bright and glorious.

Thank you for our loving friends
And family members dear.
O hear our joyful songs of praise
This thankful time of year.

~Psalm 100~

Make a joyful noise unto the Lord, all ye lands.

Serve the Lord with gladness: come before His presence with singing.

Know ye that the Lord he is God: it is He that

hath made us, and not we ourselves;

We are His people, and the sheep of His pasture.

Enter into His gates with thanksgiving, and into His courts with praise:

Be thankful unto Him, and bless His name.

For the Lord is good; His mercy is everlasting;

And His truth endureth to all generations.

Thanksgiving Prayer

T   Thank you, Lord, for bounties sweet, as

H   Happy hearts together meet.

A   All our praise to Thee we give

N   Near our hearts, may thy Spirit live.

K   King of life, Savior, and Friend,

S   Salvation's gift your death did send.

G   Giving freely to all, a choice;

I   In Heaven's gates the saved rejoice.

V   Voices sing with heartfelt praise

I   Inviting Christ to guide our ways.

N   Never sleeping, God alone…

G   Grant us safety as earth we roam.

P   Pressing on 'til that blessed day, we'll

R   Rest in the glory of Heaven's bright ray

A   Always, will we laud Thy name,

Y   Yaweh, Father, still the same.

E   Ever keep us in Thy care;

R   Remember our Thanksgiving Prayer!

~Psalm 118: 24~

This is the day which the Lord hath made;

we will rejoice and be glad in it.

Daybreak After a Winter Storm

There is a hush of solitude
In the dank and dreary air.
Trees are plated with crystals.
The weather is far from fair.

The harsh wind, now subsided,
Leaves disorder in its path.
Fallen tree limbs are strewn about—
Creatures quake in the aftermath.

The birdhouse feeder is emptied.
Seeds are scattered across the snow.
The children's sleds have drifted
To where—no one can know!

Temperatures dip below zero.
It's a cold and lifeless morn.
But the gloom of night must bid farewell
As a bright new day is born.

~Matthew 28:5-6~

And the angel answered and said unto the women, Fear not

ye: for I know that ye seek Jesus, which was crucified.

He is not here: for He is risen as He said.

Come, see the place where the Lord lay.

Christ Has Risen

C   Come and see the empty grave

H   He has risen our souls to save!

R   Remember how He preached and taught

I   In the temple, men's souls He sought.

S   Savior of mankind is He;

T   Trust Him for eternity.

H   He has conquered death's cold sting

A   And lives again, triumphant King.

S   Souls no longer need be sad—

R   Rejoice, ye Christians! Be ye glad!

I   In heaven, now, Christ's glory is shown,

S   Sitting on God's right hand throne.

E   Eternal joy's forever ours

N   Now Christ wields unvanquished powers.

~Revelation 19:1, 2a, 4~

And after these things I heard a great voice

of much people in heaven saying,

Alleluia;

Salvation, and glory, and honor, and power,

Unto the Lord our God:

For true and righteous are His judgments:

And the four and twenty elders and the

four and twenty beasts fell down and

worshipped God that sat on the

throne, saying, Amen; Alleluia.

Hallelujah

H   Hallelujah! Christ arose!

A   Although the stealth of evil foes

L   Led Him to a cruel cross;

L   Led the world to painful loss.

E   Emerging from a cold, dark grave…

L   Lives the conquering Christ to save.

U   Urge each one to praise and sing

J   Judah's mighty Lion King.

A   Alleluia! Heaven's song

H   Hail Him now, ye happy throng!

~Song of Solomon 2:11-12~

For, lo, the winter is past, the rain is over and gone;

The flowers appear on the earth;

the time of the singing of birds is come,

and the voice of the turtle is heard in our land.

Hark! The Robin Sings

Just a few short weeks ago
The ground was covered with white snow.
The sky was filled with crystal flakes,
While fields displayed cold, frozen lakes.

But today a distant sound
Comes echoing across the ground.
A sound of joyful, springtime cheer
Flitters to my listening ear.

While robin sweetly sings her verse,
Rebirth of life appears on earth.
Buds and leaves the trees do fill,
As bunnies scamper up the hill.

Fields, once brown, are now bright green.
It truly is a wondrous scene.
Hark! The robin sweetly sings
And spreads the news on outstretched wings.

~Psalm 104:10, 12-14, 16, 17~

He sendeth the springs into the valleys, which run among the hills.

By them shall the fowls of the heaven have their
habitation, which sing among the branches.

He watereth the hills from his chambers: the earth
is satisfied with the fruit of thy works.

He causeth the grass to grow for the cattle, and herb for the
service of man: that he may bring forth food out of the earth;

The trees of the Lord are full of sap; the cedars
of Lebanon, which He planted;

Where the birds make their nests: as for the
stork, the fir trees are her house.

Springtime Surprise

It's April tenth and
    spring's been here
        for more than twenty days.

The sunshine bright has
    warmed the earth
        with brilliant yellow rays.

Birds have started
    building nests
        in bushes and tall trees.

The branches swaying
    in the woods
        show just a hint of breeze.

Dear little wren
    outside my house
        chirps with a questioning eye…

The entire world
    seems upside down;
        there's a snowstorm in the sky!

~Revelation 21:23-24~

And the city had no need of the sun,

neither of the moon, to shine in it:

the glory of God did lighten it,

and the Lamb is the light thereof.

Spring Fever

The things I ought to do today
I do not want to do!
How can I when the air's so warm,
And the sky's an azure blue?

The winter months have been so long—
Filled with snow and ice and chill.
All I want to do today
Is wander up the hill.

The dishes need a washing;
The laundry must be hung.
What I'd really rather do…
Is frolic in the sun!

~Psalm 8:1, 3-9~

O Lord our Lord, how excellent is thy name in all the earth!

Who hast set thy glory above the heavens.

When I consider thy heavens, the work of thy fingers,

the moon and the stars which thou hast ordained;

What is man, that thou art mindful of him? And
the son of man, that thou visitest him?

For thou hast made him a little lower than the angels,

And has crowned him with glory and honor.

Thou madest him to have dominion over the works of
thy hands; thou hast put all things under his feet:

All sheep and oxen, yea, and the beasts of the field;

The fowl of the air, and the fish of the sea, and whatsoever
passeth through the paths of the seas.

O Lord our Lord, how excellent is Thy name in all the earth!

School Year Reflections

It wasn't very long ago
    that school was just beginning.
Lunches packed and book bags filled,
    expectant faces grinning.

September came with harvest days,
    the autumn sun aglow.
The majesty of God's great power
    everywhere did show.

Showered by October leaves with
    tints of reds and golds,
The beauty of each hill and vale—
    God's perfect plan unfolds.

November and December found us
    praising our Creator
For bounties He had blessed us with
    and most of all our Savior.

January brought new horizons
    as a brand new year began.
Ever listening, ever learning,
    each day a brand new plan.

February brought to remembrance
    Christ's love beyond compare.
As we pledge our love to others
    God's greatest gift we share.

March and April, spring's appearance,
    made winter snows thaw out.
Hope of life's new, young beginning—
    buds and blossoms sprout.

May and June, spring's crown of glory,
    shed brightness, warmth, and beauty.
Each little flower and bird that sings
    reveal God's faithful duty.

Our school year now is over as
    our tears mix joy with sadness.
One thought will never leave our heart—
    having loved and shared brought gladness!

~Ephesians 4:11, 12~

And He gave some, apostles;

and some, prophets; and some, evangelists;

and some, pastors and teachers;

For the perfecting of the saints,

for the work of the ministry,

for the edifying of the body of Christ:

A Special Teacher

God chooses special people
To teach the younger crowd.
Their voices must be sure and firm;
But never get too loud.

      They know just how important
      That first, loose tooth can be.
      They understand and comfort
      Fears that worry constantly.

Even when things go awry,
Teacher won't despair.
Her gentle words of kindness
Spread loving warmth and care.

      The classroom pet may get away—
      Milk splatter to the floor;
      But Teacher takes all this in stride
      To soothe a heart that's sore.

Some days, goals seem so futile
When it comes to A-B-C's.
Reading lessons aren't completed;
For Teacher's patching skinned knees

School is more than letters, though—
Or counting to one hundred.
It's learning how to work and share
With classmates and with kindred.

Yes, God chooses special people
To nurture, teach, and train,
The young ones in the classroom
Where gentle ways must reign.

Thank you, Dearest Teacher,
You are that special one,
Who taught not only school books—
But to love and praise God's Son.

~Proverbs 7: 1-3~

My son, keep my words, and lay up my commandments with thee.

Keep my commandments, and live; and my law as the apple of thine eye.

Bind them upon they fingers, write them upon the table of thine heart.

~Psalm 119: 105~

Thy word is a lamp unto my feet, and a light unto my path.

~ Luke 11:28b~

Blessed are they that hear The Word of God, and keep it.

To the Christian School Graduate

Your graduation's here at last.
It's difficult to believe—
That from these halls of learning,
You've earned the right to leave.

Don't forget the treasures you've learned
Nor the precious sayings you've heard.
Most of all—hide deep in your heart
The gems from God's Holy Word.

May our Lord's sure, gentle guidance
Be a lamp unto your feet.
May you rely upon His power
With each circumstance you meet.

The journey of life is not easy;
There will be struggles along the way.
So...let God's strength be a comfort to you;
Let His love and joy guide each day.

~Matthew 8:23-26~

And when He was entered into a ship, His disciples followed Him.

And behold, there arose a great tempest in the sea, insomuch
that the ship was covered with waves: but He was asleep.

And His disciples came to Him, and awoke Him, saying,

Lord save us: we perish.

And He saith unto them, Why are ye fearful, O ye of little faith? Then
He arose, and rebuked the winds and the sea; and there was a great calm.

Seaside Adventures

~Isaiah 43:1, 2a~

But now thus saith the LORD that created thee, O Jacob, and he that formed thee, O Israel, Fear not: for I have redeemed thee, I have called thee by thy name; thou art mine.

When thou passest through the waters, I will be with thee; and through the rivers, they shall not overflow thee:

~ Psalm 93:4~

The Lord on high is mightier than the noise of many waters, yea, than the mighty waves of the sea.

~Psalm 104:24-27~

O Lord, how manifold are thy works! In wisdom hast thou made them all: the earth is full of thy riches.

So is this great and wide sea, wherein are things creeping innumerable, both small and great beasts. There go the ships: there is that leviathan, whom thou hast made to play therein.

Ocean Playground

Growing up in South Jersey, I was privileged as a youngster to have many eventful trips to Ocean City. I fondly recall walking the sand with my parents and sister. My beach pail and shovel were my tools. I cheerfully anticipated and envisioned the next magnificent sand castle we would fashion from the damp seashore beneath our feet.

We would search out just the right spot to spread our blanket…not too close to the water's edge; but close enough so we could take a quick dip to cool off when castle building became too hot and wearisome.

My favorite waves were the smooth flowing hills that I could glide over with the slightest effort. The fierce and foamy white waves were not my favorite. I had had too many experiences of tumbling underwater as crashing waves broke over my head. The ocean's strength could be scary. I continue to leave surfing to those of more adventurous spirit.

Little did I know, as I played along the Atlantic seaboard of the Jersey shore, that one day I would find myself living near this great ocean once again. This time, however, over five hundred miles north. How different the rocky coastline of Maine is compared to the flat playground of the mid-Atlantic states. The thundering sea spray pelting the rocks and sea life in its wake reveals the power of the mighty ocean. In turn, I am reminded of the One whose power controls this raging of the sea. Come with me as I reminisce my seaside adventures!

~Psalm 89:8, 9~

O Lord of Hosts, who is a strong Lord unto Thee?

or to Thy faithfulness round about thee?

Thou rulest the raging of the sea: when the waves

thereof arise, thou stillest them.

By the Sea

As rays of sunlight overhead
Warm my wind tossed hair,
I gaze upon the ocean waves
Amid a day so fair.

Sailing ships and motorboats
Rock on lulling waves,
While sea life creatures take a turn
Investigating caves.

The lapping waves rush rock and sand
And seek an inlet cove,
Leaving pools of briny sea
Where snails and minnows rove.

Screeching seagulls fill the air
With raucous searing tones,
Swooping down to search for food
Among the rocks and stones.

Nature's call is strong, today,
It tugs at my inmost self.
The sun, the waves, the birds in flight,
Paint portraits of God-given wealth.

~Psalm 95:3-5~

For the Lord is a great God, and a great King above all gods.

In His hand are the deep places of the earth:
the strength of the hills is His also.

The sea is His, and He made it; and His hands formed the dry land.

Seascape

I strained as far as my eyes could see
And watched the seagulls flying free,
Above the thundering ocean's roar,
In graceful rhythm their wings did soar.

I gazed upon the foaming waves
Crashing against the rocky caves,
While sprays of misty ocean dew
Splashed back upon the waters blue.

Amid the land, the sky, the sea,
A marvelous thought arouses me.
Knowing my Lord has made them all,
His majestic powers my heart does enthrall!

~Psalm 98:5-9a~

Sing unto the Lord with the harp; with the harp,
and the voice of a psalm.

With trumpets and sound of cornet make a
joyful noise before the Lord, the King.

Let the sea roar, and the fullness thereof; the
world, and they that dwell therein.

Let the floods clap their hands: let the hills be
joyful together--Before the Lord;

Seashore Symphony

Lapping waves against the shore
    Spray the sun-bleached sand.
Children's laughter fills the air
    As they scamper o'er the land.

Seagulls spread their flapping wings
    Screeching as they fly...
Turning, twisting through the air;
    Filling the daytime sky.

Tiny crabs and large ones, too
    Side step through the foam,
Shells a crackling with each step—
    They inch their way towards home.

Gentle winds brush waving grasses.
    They whisper through rock and cove.
Nature's singing by the ocean—
    Where sea creatures ramble and rove.

~Luke 19:9-10~

And Jesus said unto him,
This day is salvation come to this house,
forsomuch as he also is a son of Abraham.

For the Son of man is come to seek
and to save that which was lost.

~John 3:17~

For God sent not his Son into the world
To condemn the world; but that the world
through Him might be saved.

The Lighthouse

Across the cozy harbor cove
Stands a symbol of hope and light.
The lighthouse beams are all aglow;
Giving guidance and safety tonight.

Its rays of light reveal the snares
Of rocks that cross man's path.
The faithful beams make seaways safe
From storm and waves' cruel wrath.

There is another Lighthouse tall
That saves and guides man's soul.
A Beacon that overrides his fate;
The plan of salvation…God's goal.

'Tis Christ, the Lighthouse in oceans dark
Who guides men o'er life's stormy waves.
Rest your eyes on the Savior today;
Look to Jesus, the Lighthouse that saves.

~Isaiah 7:14~

Therefore the Lord himself
shall give you a sign;

Behold, a virgin shall conceive, and bear a Son,

And shall call his name Immanuel.

Christmas Tidings

~Luke 2:11~

For unto you is born this day In the city of David
a Saviour, which is Christ the Lord.

✻

Reviewing the Year

Christmas for most of us is a time of wonder. Brilliant colored lights adorn the fragrant smelling evergreen trees. Beautifully wrapped gifts add excitement to the special day. Family and friends gather around the table feasting on favorite recipes, but mostly on cherished memories. It is the time of year when joy overcomes gloom and sharing outweighs selfishness. The birth of one Holy Child made it all possible.

While honoring and celebrating Christ's birth, I cannot help but to reflect on the events of the year gone by in my own family's journey. This time of year, for me, has become the time to praise the Lord for safely and faithfully guiding us through another 365 days of life's daily ups and downs.

When our household included only two children, our first computer made an entrance into my husband's office. With the new ease of quickly printing out multiple documents, our first annual Christmas letter became reality. Each year our letter included a paragraph or two about each individual member. It was fun to relive the milestones of each member's achievements. With the addition of each bundle of joy, a special thrill would fill my heart as I announced each new birth. I noted the weight, length, hair and eye color of this new little one, so uniquely and beautifully fashioned by God the Creator.

How thrilled God the Father must have been when His angels announced the birth of His only begotten Son! We weren't told in scripture the color of Jesus' eyes or how long He was at birth. We do know His birth was unique. He was born in a stable and welcomed by humble shepherds. Not exactly the expected beginning for the ruler of the world. God's ways are higher than man's ways. He has proven time and again that He is the master designer. He can take the low and downtrodden and lift them up to high places of wealth, wisdom, and authority. Abraham, Joseph, and Solomon, are examples of the many patriarchs, governors, and kings proclaimed in the Bible. These men and many others were assigned (and accomplished) amazing tasks by God's will and design. Their lives were testaments to God's power and what He can do if the vessel is willing to be led by the Lord.

As our family Christmas letters continued each year, I decided to add an extra touch to its contents in the form of poetry. The Christmas poems from these annual reports now fill the Christmas Tidings section of this book.

✳

~ *John 15:12, 13* ~

This is my commandment, that ye love one
another, as I have loved you.

~ *I John 4:19* ~

We love Him, because He first loved us.

He First Loved Us

He loved us unconditionally.
    He left His home on high.
He sacrificed His wealth and fame
    To come to earth to die.

The Holy Babe of Bethle'm town
    Was born in a stable crude.
The only ones to welcome Him—
    Shepherds and cattle rude.

How can we thank this Gentle Child
    Who came to set us free?
How can we show our gratitude
    To the Christ of Calvary?

Let us offer words--of love and joy--
    To neighbors far and near.
Let us share the Christmas Story
    At this Blessed time of year.

✳

~Luke 2:7~

And she brought forth her firstborn son, and wrapped
him in swaddling clothes, and laid Him in a manger;
because there was no room for them in the inn.

Heaven's Gift

The King has come! Heaven's angels declare.
Sweet music rings through the starlit air.

Lo, in a Bethlehem manger stall,
Mary soothes Jesus, kind ruler of all.

Praise Him, adore Him on bended knee.
"I Am" of all ages come set us free.

This dear Christmas gift from heaven above,
Is sent with God's blessings ~ wrapped in His Love.

~Luke 2:8-17~

And there were in the same country shepherds abiding in
the field, keeping watch over their flock by night.

And, lo, the angel of the Lord came upon them, and the glory of
the Lord shone round about them: and they were sore afraid.

And the angel said unto them, Fear not: for, behold, I bring
you good tidings of great joy, which shall be to all people.

For unto you is born this day in the city of David
a Savior, which is Christ the Lord.

And this shall be a sign unto you; Ye shall find the babe
wrapped in swaddling clothes, lying in a manger.

And suddenly there was with the angel a multitude of
the heavenly host praising God, and saying,

Glory to God in the highest and on earth peace, good will toward men.

And it came to pass, as the angels were gone away from
them into heaven, the shepherds said one to another,

Let us now go even unto Bethlehem, and see this thing which
is come to pass, which the Lord hath made known unto us.

And they came with haste, and found Mary, and
Joseph, and the babe lying in a manger.

And when they had seen it, they made known abroad the
saying which was told them concerning this child.

And all they that heard it wondered at those things
which were told them by the shepherds.

God's Greatest Gift

G   God made this world of beauty,
O   Of land and sky and sea.
D   Down from His throne of glory,
'S   Sent His Son to set us free.

G   God showered Earth with blessings;
R   Revealed a bright new day;
E   Extended grace to humankind,
A   And love to guide the way.
T   The infant child of Mary,
E   Eternal Hope, His birth proclaims.
S   Shepherds spread the story—
T   Told the world of Christ who reigns.

G   God shared His only offspring.
I   In sacrifice, He gave His all—
F   For a desperate world of sinners
T   That the lost might heed Christ's call.

※

~Isaiah 61:1-2~

The Spirit of the Lord God is upon me; because the Lord hath anointed me to preach good tidings unto the meek; he hath sent me to bind up the brokenhearted, to proclaim liberty to the captives, and the opening of the prison to them that are bound;

To proclaim the acceptable year of the Lord, and the day of vengeance of our God; to comfort all that mourn.

Christmas Tidings

C   Carols echo through the air.

H   Harken to the news they bear.

R   Ring the bells of Heaven above;

I   In Christ, there's everlasting love.

S   Sing ye, carolers, in the snow.

T   Tell of that day so long ago.

M   Merrily sing the ancient story

A   And honor, now, the King of Glory.

S   Sweetly, Christmas hymns retell—

T   The royal birth of Israel.

I   In that lowly manger stall

D   Did God send hope, for sinners, all!

I   Inside our hearts, God's mercy has blessed

N   No longer burdened, frail souls can rest.

G   Give praise to God for Christ is born!

S   Send forth the Word from night 'til morn.

~Matthew 2:1-5, 8-11~

Now when Jesus was born in Bethlehem of Judea in the days of Herod
the king, behold, there came wise men from the east to Jerusalem,

Saying, Where is he that is born King of the Jews? for we have
seen his star in the east, and are come to worship Him.

When Herod the king had heard these things, he
was troubled, and all Jerusalem with him.

And when he had gathered all the chief priests and Scribes of the
people together, he demanded of them where Christ should be born.

And they said unto him, In Bethlehem of Judaea: for thus it is written
by the prophet, And he sent them to Bethlehem, and said, Go and
search diligently for the young child; and when ye have found him,
bring me word again, that I may come and worship him also.

When they had heard the king, they departed; and, lo,
the star, which they saw in the east, went before them, till
it came and stood over where the young child was.

When they saw the star, they rejoiced with exceeding great joy.

And when they were come into the house, they saw the young
child with Mary his mother, and fell down, and worshipped
him: and when they had opened their treasures, they presented
unto him gifts; gold, and frankincense, and myrrh.

Love Came Down From Heaven

Love came down from Heaven
When Jesus Christ was born.
Mary, Joseph, and the world
Were blessed by God that morn.

Love came down from Heaven
God's Heavenly choir sang.
Angels told the story;
The starlit hillsides rang.

Love came down from Heaven
When Christ was sent to earth.
Kind shepherds came to worship
At His lowly manger birth.

Love came down from Heaven
On that night so long ago.
A special star led Wise Men
To the place God's Son did grow.

Love came down from Heaven,
'Tis a story sweet and true.
The Christ Child sent from Heaven
Came to rescue me and you.

~*Matthew* 1:22-23~

Now all this was done, that it might be
fulfilled which was spoken of the Lord by the
prophet, saying,

Behold, a virgin shall be with child, and shall bring forth a son,
and they shall call his name Emmanuel,
which being interpreted is, God with us.

Christy Has Come!

C   Cradled in a manger stall

H   Heralded by the angels' call

R   Redeemer of Jews and Gentiles alike

I   Is Baby Jesus this Christmas night.

S   Shepherds adore the infant mild;

T   Then tell the world of the Holy Child.

H   Heaven to earthly men has bent

A   As new hope and joy to earth is sent.

S   So let us come on bended knee;

C   Come to the manger the King to see.

O   Oh, worship the One who conquers sin

M   Messiah is He, if your heart He is in.

E   Emmanuel, the Lord of our life

!   Protect us now from sin and strife.

✳

II Corinthians 5:17-18

Therefore if any man be in Christ, he is a new creature: old things are passed away; behold, all things are become new.

And all things are of God, who hath reconciled us to himself by Jesus Christ, and hath given to us the ministry of reconciliation;

✳

Christmas Sounds

C   Carolers lift their voices in song.

H   Horse drawn sleighs tote singers along.

R   Ringing bells waft joy to our ears;

I   Immortal tunes spread hope through the years.

S   Sing, ye choirs, of Jesus' birth.

T   Tell of the One come down to earth.

M   Miracle Child, infant so mild,

A   Atonement, now, is reconciled.

S   Savior of mankind is He.

S   Savior of sinners like you and me.

O   Only Son of the Father on High,

U   Unveils God's glory in a manger sty.

N   Now peace and joy shall overflow.

D   Death's sting no longer will be sin's blow.

S   Songs of victory reel through the air—
     Over creation: we're freed from sin's snare.

✳

~Luke 21:36~

Watch ye therefore, and pray always, that ye may be
accounted worthy to escape all these things that shall
come to pass, and to stand before the Son of man.

~I Thessalonians 5:17, 18~

Pray without ceasing.

In everything give thanks: for this is the will of
God in Christ Jesus concerning you.

~I Timothy 2: 1-3, 8~

I exhort therefore, that, first of all, supplications, prayers,
intercessions, and giving of thanks, be made for all men;

For kings, and for all that are in authority; that we may lead
a quiet and peaceable life in all godliness and honesty.

For this is good and acceptable in the sight of God our Saviour…

I will therefore that men pray every where, lifting up
holy hands, without wrath and doubting.

Christmas Prayer

O Christmas Star, you shine so bright.
You tell us of that Holy Night
When Christ was born so long ago,
Amid the stable and manger low.

O Christmas Star, your Heavenly glow
Tells of the love God's mercy did show—
Grace that transcends man's lowly plight;
Peace that endures through the lonely night.

Thank you, Dear Father, for Heaven's gift;
Upward to Thee, our faces we lift.
Help us be worthy of the love you bestow,
As life's journey we travel on earth here below.

~Isaiah 9:6~

For unto us a child is born, unto us a son is given: and the government shall be upon his shoulder: and his name shall be called Wonderful, Counsellor, The mighty God, The everlasting Father, The Prince of Peace.

~ *Matthew 1:21* ~

And she shall bring forth a son, and thou shalt call his name JESUS: for He shall save his people from their sins.

Call His Name Jesus

Christmas time's arrived once more
The Angels sing their song.
Shepherds kneel in quietness
There is no clamoring throng.

The Babe of Bethlehem was born
On a starlit wintry night.
The unsuspecting world of man
Was blessed with Heaven's Light.

Thou shalt call His name Jesus;
Joseph's instructions were clear.
He shall save his people
From the curse of sin and fear.

Wonderful, Counsellor, Mighty God,
The prophet foretold it true.
Everlasting Father of all—
Came to redeem the world anew.

Dear Prince of Peace, we offer praise
For the blessing you did bestow,
Upon our needy, sinful world,
On that night so long ago.

JESUS is still the reason for this season!!!

Children's Corner
~ A Precious Parcel of Poems for and about children ~

~Matthew 19: 13, 14~

Then were there brought unto him little children, that he should put his hands on them, and pray: and the disciples rebuked them.

But Jesus said, Suffer little children, and forbid them not, to come unto me: for of such is the kingdom of heaven.

When I Grow Up

"When I Grow Up I Want to Be a Teacher." That was the title of an essay I wrote in ninth grade. I can still remember the reasons for this decision. The assignment was one of those exercises where you list all the reasons why you don't want to achieve the goal and conclude with the real reason the particular goal was chosen.

I began my essay by sharing that I didn't want to be a teacher just because my mother, my grandfather, my aunt, and my great aunt were all teachers. Of course, having so many teachers in the family certainly had a lasting influence; but that wasn't what drew me to this profession.

Other "not why" reasons that I listed were being able to write on the chalkboard, placing shiny and colorful stickers on well done papers and tests, and taking exciting field trips with the students. These were all activities that to a then, fourteen year old student, might be 'pretty cool', but still were not the real reasons I desired this profession.

Attending Christian school the first seven years of my life put me in contact with some of the sweetest teachers I have ever known. I loved school. I am sure it was the nurturing and care of these wonderful teachers that helped shape my life and set me on my journey. With this foundation, I looked forward to sharing what I had learned with others, especially children.

My church experiences were also influential in shaping my path. My first opportunity to teach was during Vacation Bible School. How excited I was to attend my first teachers' meeting and be assigned to a fourth grade class. How important I felt sitting among the other experienced teachers, including my mom, and learning the details and plans for the upcoming ministry. This experience sold me on the path of teaching...Teacher's Education 101 here I come!

Student teaching during my final semester of college was awesome. I loved working with children. Since music was also a special part of me, I included it wherever I could in my lesson plans. Singing songs like "Itsy Bitsy Spider" and "B-I-N-G-O" were always at the top of the list and still provide fond memories.

A child's world is one of wonder and questions; one of hearing and experiencing brand new ideas for the first time. In the classroom, they learn how to express their thoughts and feelings among children and teachers. That is a big step outside the comfort of family and home; it is one of the first steps of independence.

That is why I wanted to be a teacher! I wanted to be the adult standing by, watching and guiding the precious young lives in my care. I wanted to be the one witnessing the growth as each child blossomed into the special person God intended them to become. That was my motivation to becoming a teacher!

I praise the Lord for His guidance in my choice of a teaching profession. It has been my joy to have had over 500 students pass through my classroom doors or sit under my tutelage at the piano. That also includes homeschooling each of my own five children.

Having invested many years in teaching children, I found it brought another rewarding benefit—the wealth of experiences and material that motivated me to write poetry. The following poems are dedicated to all my students and my own children who through the years reminded me how to think and understand as a child!

I have no greater joy than to hear that my children walk in truth. ~ III John 4

~I Corinthians 13:11~

When I was a child,

I spake as a child, I understood as a child,

I thought as a child...

The Season of Summer

The Season of Summer is here again,
The trees are fully clothed
In fresh green leaves and robin nests;
Lawns just recently mowed.

Back yard gardens are planted.
Beans begin to sprout.
Carrots, beets, and potatoes
Are a few more plants poking out.

Flowers, abloom in the sunlight,
Invite bees and butterflies—come!
Squirrels leave their nests in the treetops
To frolic and play in the sun.

Meadows are sprinkled with children,
Who laugh as they run to and fro.
The season of summer's upon us.
Hearts are happy and faces aglow!

Showtime

It's Showtime out our window.
Sneaky squirrel is having lunch.
He's up to his old tricks again
On the birdseeds he does munch.

He scoots atop the feeder roof,
Spying seeds along the floor;
Pokes and claws to reach them,
Then he looks around for more.

He sees us in our kitchen,
Watching his every move.
That doesn't bother frisky squirrel—
This food robber's very smooth!

Chipmunk Lunch

There was a little chipmunk
That ran across my roof.
He'd just finished eating,
From our little birdseed booth.

His face was full of goodies;
His cheeks were bulging lumps.
It really seemed this chipmunk
Had taken ill with mumps!

Dear Butterfly

Dear Butterfly, you flit right by
the flowers on my sill.
You seem in such a hurry
as you flutter toward the hill.

Your spotted wings of orange and black
spread gracefully through the air;
But your swiftness as you hustle by
shows lack of time to spare.

Is your family waiting for your
day's work to be done?
Or, have you just decided
to quit early for some fun?

I doubt that I will ever know
the answers to this quiz.
Your wings just keep on flitting
as behind my house you whiz!

Favorite Toys

Little girls and little boys
Love to play with favorite toys.
Little girls have Dolly Dear
To cuddle, feed, and dry her tear.

Girls just love to have a tea; or
Pretend they're on a shopping spree.
Dress up time is so much fun
For strolling baby in the sun.

Little boys have fire trucks,
Bows and arrows to shoot large bucks.
Race cars, horses, cowboy hats—
Don't forget those baseball bats.

Riding bikes is an all-time thrill,
Especially when it's down a hill.
Little girls and little boys
Love to play with favorite toys.

Night Winds

The sky is dark
    The moon is bright.
The howling wind
    Does blow tonight!

It scratches at
    The window screens
And makes the most
    Annoying screams.

The woodland trees
    Do groan and shake,
As north winds sweep
    The frozen lake.

Ruffle feathered
    Birds withdraw
Within their nests
    Of twigs and straw.

Squirrels hole up
    In knotted trees,
While chipmunks
    Burrow from the breeze.

The wind does blow;
    The house does quake.
The night time wind
    Keeps me awake!

Windy Day

The wind is blowing all around.
It blows the leaves across the ground.
It swings the swing in my backyard.
The wind is blowing very hard.

It makes the trees to bend and twist.
It knocked the kite string off my wrist.
The hat that once was on my head
Is over in the flower bed.

The clothes are flapping on the line.
That shirt which flew away was mine!
The wind is blowing hard today.
I wish that it would blow away!

Someone at My Window

There is someone at my window
With a small black cap.
He isn't very big at all
As he gives a little tap.

Tap, tap here. Tap, tap there.
What's he hunting for?
Could it be the little seeds
Fallen to the window floor?

Have you guessed this someone's name
Who is trying to invade?
It is Black-Capped Chickadee
Dining in the shade!

Ladybird Beetle

There is a little ladybug
That lives inside my house.
She climbs upon the curtains—
Much quieter than a mouse.

She likes to sit on leaves of plants;
The aphids she does eat.
Each morning I can see her fly
To find her favorite treat.

Sometimes she likes to cling to lamps,
Or on the ceiling wall.
When I look up to see her there
I fear that she may fall.

Ladybug is quite at home
Flitting through the air.
I really need not worry
For she likes to fly up there.

Noisy Critter

There is a noisy critter
        chirping in my room.

I have searched in every nook,
        poking with my broom.

Successfully escaping--
        everywhere I gaze,

This racket he is making
        could last for days and days.

Maybe if I'm quiet
        and hold my breath real tight,

This cricket in my bedroom
        will sleep all through the night!

Mr. Robin

Mr. Robin, in my yard,
You are looking very hard,
For a tasty, springtime treat
Living 'neath your tiny feet.

You can't seem to see him there
Even though you strain and stare;
But soon you'll hear a little worm
Beneath the soil, stretch and squirm.

With such care, you cock your head
To hear the worm that's still in bed.
Quickly now, with lightning speed,
Your strong, sharp beak has done its deed.

Bird Feeder Frenzy

The invitation came by sky
As Mother Robin flapped on high.
Mrs. Squirrel heard the news
And chattered like she'd blown a fuse.

Sister chipmunk figured out
What the news was all about.
She told her family that a feast
Awaited them two blocks due east.

As they scampered down the street,
Each dreamed of goodies, soon they'd eat!
Now, passing by a little stream;
A noonday meal they hoped to glean.

By the time the crowd arrived,
Three dozen birds were easily spied.
A gathering of feathered friends
Was perched on feeders tips to ends.

Curious bunnies came to see
What the clamor seemed to be.
Once the mystery was known,
Each scurried back to his own home.

Big birds, small birds were pecking hard
At the bird feeders in my yard.
Blackbirds, blue jays, goldfinches, too,
Made more noise than a real live zoo!

Bird seeds, sunflower seeds and more
Filled to the brim, my feeders four.
What a ruckus did occur!
My backyard feeders caused quite a stir!

Bubbles

Bubbles, bubbles in the air
Flying here and flying there.
Bubbles, bubbles make no sound
Floating gently to the ground.

I wave my wand across the breeze
And watch the bubbles fly with ease.
Circles of purple, red, and blue
Make hours of fun for me and you.

The Clouds are Passing By

High clouds, low clouds,
Heavy clouds and light clouds,
White clouds, dark clouds,
The clouds are passing by.

Rain clouds, fluffy clouds,
Skinny clouds, puffy clouds,
Clouds are floating pictures
High up in the sky.

Cat clouds, dog clouds,
Pony clouds and fish clouds,
Dragon clouds in castles
Make nervous maidens cry.

Soft clouds, wispy clouds,
Cold clouds and gray clouds,
Foggy clouds on picnic days
Make my family sigh!

Raindrops

Raindrops running down my roof
Scurry to and fro.
They bump into each other
At my small window.

Droplets from the sky above
Bounce off oak tree leaves;
Trickle down the chimney stone
Across the house top eaves.

Falling, falling from the clouds,
Plopping to the ground;
Small, cool drops of water
Make such a pleasant sound!

Mr. Scarecrow

Hello, Mr. Scarecrow standing all alone. Garden crops are harvested;

Birds and bunnies have gone home!

Summer days are over; harvesting is done. There's no more work for Scarecrow—

He's dancing in the sun!

Snow Crystals

Have you ever stopped and wondered
At the snowflakes in the sky?
Have you ever watched them twinkling
As they hurtle past your eye?

Have you stood in sheer amazement
As they glisten like fresh dew?
Have you gazed upon their beauty
As they flitter around you?

Snowflakes, crystals, diamonds,
Whate'er may be their name—
I'm glad they fell to earth tonight
To please and entertain!

Bedtime

When I go to bed at night
My Mom turns on a little light.
It will keep me safe and sound
While to sleepy land I'm bound.

Sometimes the wind makes windows rattle.
It sounds to me like pounding cattle;
But Mommy says I need not fear
For she and Dad are very near.

~Proverbs 25:11-13~

A word fitly spoken is like apples of gold in pictures of silver.

As an earring of gold, and an ornament of fine gold,
so is a wise reprover upon an obedient ear.

As the cold of snow in the time of harvest, so is a faithful messenger
to them that send him: for he refresheth the soul of his masters.

~Psalm 104:33,34~

I will sing unto the Lord as long as I live: I will sing
praise to my God while I have my being.

My meditation of him shall be sweet: I will be glad in the Lord.

Reflections

~ *Psalm 77: 1, 6, 11-12, 14* ~

I cried unto God with my voice, even unto God
with my voice; and he gave ear unto me.

I call to remembrance my song in the night: I commune with
mine own heart: and my spirit made diligent search.

I will remember the works of the Lord: surely
I will remember thy wonders of old.

I will meditate also of all thy work, and talk of thy doings.

Thou art the God that doest wonders: thou hast
declared thy strength among the people.

~Deuteronomy 6:4-9 ~

Hear, O Israel: The Lord our God is one Lord: and
thou shalt love the Lord thy God with all thine heart,
and with all thy soul, and with all thy might.

And these words, which I command thee this day, shall be in thine heart:

And thou shalt teach them diligently unto thy children, and shalt
talk of them when thou sittest in thine house, and when thou walkest
by the way, and when thou liest down, and when thou risest up.

And thou shalt bind them for a sign upon thine hand,
and they shall be as frontlets between thine eyes.

And thou shalt write them upon the posts of thy house, and on thy gates.

An Open Letter to My Father in Heaven

Dear Heavenly Father,

I presented another poem to one of your children a few months ago. She is bravely grieving the loss of her dear husband, a Christian man, a faithful missionary, a father of young children, and a friend to many. The poem is simply called *Heaven*.

I marvel at this poem's creation over fifteen years ago. You were taking me on one of life's little detours. I had just had another relapse with the MS that has intermittently attacked me since 1980. As a mother of five, I felt blessed that I had stayed healthy enough to bring these young lives to a saving knowledge of your grace, but at the same time I worried--a human frailty--that I was not going to be around to see them all graduate from high school.

During the particular summer of 1996 my sensitivity to the annoying pain also seemed to leave me more sensitive to Your still, small voice. It just seemed that words kept streaming from your "Great Word Bank" in Heaven and connected with my pen in hand. Trying to be brave about the whole health issue--or lack of--I began reflecting about my coronation to Heaven one day and what it would be like up there with You and my loved ones that passed through the veil already. I even began to write my biography for my funeral service…one less detail for my family to worry about. Words kept coming and before I knew it a poem was born.

> There is a land far brighter
> Than the one we trod today.
> There is a hope far grander
> Than this world could e'er display…
> (entire poem is on page 43)

Little did I know that I would be placing Your lovingly inspired poem in a funeral bulletin for my father-in-law just four months later. In fact, OUR poem has been printed out, framed and given away dozens of times in hopes of being an encouragement to those in sorrow. With internet, I can send it to many grieving souls--unframed, but still as a messenger of Your encouragement, Your love, and Your mercy.

I've often wondered how you managed to get my attention to sit down and write poems when my little ones were still around my knee. Your plan is always so grand, though. You knew what lay ahead of me—You knew my kidney disease would slow me down, as it has these last two years, and that doctor appointments would monopolize my waking hours. You knew that dialysis was in my future and spurred me on to write NOW…no procrastination allowed!

Lord, I am still 'keeping on keeping on'. Words from Heaven still find my listening ears. In fact, the Christmas poem, *Heaven's Gift*, you gave me yesterday was a special blessing ~ You are so Faithful! Lord, You are my strength!

The King has come!
Heaven's angels declare.
Sweet music rings
Through the starlit air.
(entire poem is on page 119)

Father, thank You for Your gift of language. Thank You for the Bible which is filled with words and scenes that You want us to learn from. It is Your words that inspire the writer to write, the singer to sing, the musician to play. It is Your Word that encourages us to carry on, even in the face of life's biggest struggles and disappointments. This is because Your Word tells the story of Jesus, the One who understands the very sadness and challenges that Your children face daily. He left His home in glory to conquer death, so that we could live again with You some day in Heaven. That is what Your story is all about!

Lord, please continue to use my weakened vessel as a pathway for Your words to resonate through; that others may be uplifted and encouraged. In the words of the Savior:

"Thy kingdom come...Thy will be done."

Love always,

Mary

Healing Miracles of Jesus Christ

Recipient	Matthew	Mark	Luke	John
Official's son				4:46-54
Possessed man		1:21-27	4:33-37	
Peter's in-law	8:14-15	1:29-31	4:38-39	
Many at sunset	8:16-17	1:32-39	4:40-41	
Leper	8:1-4	1:40-45	5:12-15	
Paralytic	9:1-8	2:1-12	5:18-26	
Man at Bethesda				5:1-17
Withered hand	12:9-13	3:1-6	6:6-11	
Crowd in Galilee	4:23-25			
Centurion's son	8:5-13		7:1-10	
Widow's son			7:11-17	
2 demoniacs	8:28-34	5:1-20	8:26-39	
Jairus daughter-1	9:18-19	5:22-24	8:41-42	
Unclean woman	9:20-22	5:24-34	8:49-56	
Jairus daughter-2	9:23-26	5:35-43	8:49-56	
2 blind men	9:27-31			
Dumb man	9:32-34			
Touching clothes	14:34-36	6:53-56		
Crowd in Galilee	9:35			
Few in Nazareth		6:1-6		
Gentile's daughter	15:21-28	7:24-30		
Deaf man		7:31-37		
Multitude	15:29-31			
Epileptic boy	17:14-21	9:14-29	9:37-42	
Blind man				9:1-41
Blind/dumb man	12:22-24		11:14-15	
Man of Bethsaida		8:22-26		
Stooped woman			13:10-17	
Man with Dropsy			14:1-16	
Lazarus raised				11:1-45

Ten Lepers			17:11-19	
Crowds in Judea	19:1-2			
Bartimaeus	20:29-34	10:46-52	18:35-43	
Many in Jerusalem	21:14			
Ear of Malchus			22:47-53	18:10-11
Resurrection	28:1-10	16:1-20	24:1-53	20:1-31

Other Miracles of Jesus Christ

Event	Matthew	Mark	Luke	John
Water to wine				2:1-11
1st catch of fish			5:1-11	
Calms a sea	8:23-27	4:35-41	8:22-25	
Feeds 5000	14:13-21	6:32-44	9:10-17	6:1-13
Walks on water	14:22-33	6:45-51		6:15-21
Feeds 4000	15:32-39	8:1-10		
Money in fish	17:24-27			
Tree withered	21:18-22	11:12-24		
2nd catch of fish				21:1-14

Miracles Still Happen

There are those who believe things happen by coincidence. They are probably the same ones that believe man evolved along the shores of time. I, however, have learned through experience and faith that there is One that is Greater than I. There is One that is in control of my life. He is the One that David spoke of in Psalm 119:133 when he prayed: Order my steps in thy word: and let not any iniquity have dominion over me. David also wrote: The steps of a good man are ordered by the Lord: and he delighteth in his way. (Psalm 37:23) The same God that David wrote about and prayed to, is the One that created the world and has the power to create Miracles! I believe I have experienced many miracles in my lifetime—because God has ordered my steps.

Writing has always been one of my favorite subjects. As early as second grade, I can remember writing articles for the school newspaper. By grade four, I found making up rhyming clues for treasure hunts to be a satisfying pastime. My grandfather, an avid reader of poetry, often shared his thoughts and his own writings with me when I reached high school. This interaction was a fruitful resource. Pop pop's desire to write a book, which was accomplished shortly before his death, became a motivator to me. Someday, I too, would publish a book!

College, marriage, the teaching job, children—came in quick succession. There was little down time to sit and write for pleasure, let alone write a book...until 1986. That was the first step of my miracle, although I didn't know it yet. I decided to participate in a children's writing course to hone my skill. A year later, life again intervened with our family move to another state. My writing course went on the shelf. Waiting on the Lord became my theme as I went about my teaching duties and responsibilities of wife and mother of five.

Ten years later, I restarted the writing course and managed to finish, receiving a diploma to hang in my home office. Most important was the children's story--my final assignment that concluded the course. Yes, my dream to publish a book was surely near? Rejections from queries ran high. The dream seemed further away. I kept the faith and like Lucy Maude Montgomery (*Anne of Green Gables*), filed my manuscript for the future (although not in a hat box), and waited on the Lord once again.

While waiting, teaching positions came and went. Each time I would try to befriend the art teacher at the school. I really needed to have an illustrator for my story—someone I could work with closely. In 2008 I obtained a teaching job forty-five minutes from my house! Did I really want to travel that far? Should I take this step?

Since it was classroom music and it would be only one day a week—why not? I loved music as much as writing. Having a piano in my classroom was a definite benefit. The sound of children's voices singing—another joy!

Shortly into the academic year a local author visited the school with her children's books. I purchased one for my grandchildren with the ulterior motive of checking out the book's illustrator. She was a local art teacher, but in another school district. Dare I be bold enough to take the step and contact this artist? I did. She agreed to read my manuscript. She also agreed to contract with me. It was two days before Thanksgiving—what a wonderful celebration! Thanks be to God for His unspeakable gift! By the following January my first children's book with beautiful illustrations was published.

Sometimes, God's miracles come in small steps. Sometimes those small steps turn into big miracles. What if I hadn't decided to take that writing course? What if I hadn't taken that classroom music position forty-five minutes away? What if I hadn't been bold enough to track down the children's book illustrator? What if I told you that amid the duration of this miracle, I had been dealing with multiple sclerosis as well as polycystic kidney disease and am currently undergoing dialysis three days a week? Praise be unto God, the Lord of Miracles!

> And a great multitude followed him, because they saw his
> miracles which he did on them that were diseased. ~ John 6:2

~Psalm 37:3-7~

Trust in the Lord, and do good; so shalt thou dwell
in the land, and verily thou shalt be fed.

Delight thyself also in the Lord; and He shall
give thee the desires of thine heart.

Commit thy way unto the Lord; trust also in Him; and he shall
bring it to pass. And He shall bring forth thy righteousness
as the light, and thy judgment as the noonday.

Rest in the Lord, and wait patiently for Him: Fret not
thyself because of him who prospereth in his way.

Cease from anger, and forsake wrath: fret
not thyself in any wise to do evil.

~ *Psalm 43* ~

Judge me, O God, and plead my cause against an ungodly nation: O deliver me from the deceitful and unjust man.

For thou art the God of my strength: why dost thou cast me off? Why go I mourning because of the oppression of the enemy?

O send out thy light and thy truth: let them lead me; let them bring me unto thy holy hill, and to thy tabernacles.

Then will I go unto the altar of God, unto God my exceeding joy: yea, upon the harp will I praise thee, O God my God.

Why art thou cast down, O my soul? And why art thou disquieted within me? Hope in God: for I shall yet praise him, who is the health of my countenance, and my God.

Reflections and a Poem

Todd's mom may have been a woman of slight frame, but her iron will was twice that size! I know that for two reasons.

One…I was the daughter-in-law. You know how those stories go. When I first stole Todd away from her, I could easily be intimidated. As the new relationship began to grow, understandings improved and life continued on.

Reason two…I married a Fenstermacher, and soon learned WHY she had to have an IRON WILL. I quickly put my order in for an iron will, as well!

Mother Faye was full of life, as many can attest. She always knew what she wanted to do and when. Her social calendar was a marvel to behold. She was a person of great determination and action.

There were only two times in her life that I personally know of, that really got her down. Actually, we all know of the last one…it was Alzheimer's disease—a cruel and unforgiving illness that takes one's most precious memories from its victims. Mother's iron will came in very handy in this circumstance. In spite of this major attack, she remained gracious and friendly—not all Alzheimer's patients fare so well.

The first time that I witnessed her in true distress was in 1997. She had been visiting her family out West and was on her way back home when we received an unexpected phone call from her neighbors. Her house had been broken into and several items had been stolen. Todd and I had the sad duty of sharing this information with her when we picked her up at the airport.

Later that night as we purposed to sleep in a beloved dwelling that had been a safe haven for decades—but, was now the scene of a crime—I could hear loud, overwhelming sobs coming from Mother's bedroom upstairs. As, I reflected on the events of the last 48 hours, the question WHY? came to the forefront. The following poem is the answer God blessed me with that night.

Why?

When life sometimes presents me with some
    trials too hard to bear,
I stand in my aloneness asking where's a soul
    who'll care?

Why do bad things happen to the ones who've
    done no harm?
Why does evil reap rewards, while the righteous
    reap alarm?

Why does hurt and pain o'er take the good and
    noble child;
When others far less kindly go on living lives so
    wild?

The "Why's" keep asking questions of these trials
    that hurt and wound.
No answers are forthcoming; my life seems oft'
    marooned.

Then in my deepest solitude, my Savior, I recall,
Felt much pain and agony—for my good,
    He suffered ALL.

Surprisingly my pleas of "Why" became of less
    concern,
For even my Creator bore great trials,
    harsh and stern.

Rejection, He did not deserve, not mocking
      nor distrust.
He neither should have been despised, nor have
      borne the sharp sword's thrust.

My Jesus knew His mission, and willingly
      submitted.
Yet in the midst of pain and loss the wicked He
      acquitted.

Love so abounding from my Lord, cannot be
      taken lightly.
He gave Himself for "even me"; He asked not
      "Why"? Not slightly.

He bore the cross on Calvary's Hill, my sinful
      soul to save.
His sole reward for saving me was the cruel cross
      and grave.

Praise to the Living Savior Who's prepared
      my place in glory.
The "Why's" don't really matter when I think
      of Christ's Love story!

Postscript

Do you know my Jesus? If you have read every scripture and poem in this book, you have had a great introduction to the Lord of All!

God the Creator sent His only Son, Jesus Christ to live among men and teach and preach a "better way"—God's Way. After Christ's crucifixion, resurrection, and ascension, God did not leave us comfortless. He sent His Holy Spirit to indwell those who desire to be a follower of Jesus, and one day join Him in Heaven.

Do you want to be one of Christ's followers? Do you want to go to Heaven when your days on earth are done? There is only one way to get to Heaven—that is through faith in Jesus Christ. You cannot get there because you go to church; you cannot get there because your parent's took you to Sunday school when you were young; you cannot get there because you are a "good" person and try to be honest and do right. It must be your decision. You must ask and accept Christ of your own free will. It requires the faith of a child...

✝

*For by grace, are ye saved through faith; and that
not of yourselves: it is the gift of God;*

Not of works, lest any man should boast.

~ Ephesians 2:8, 9

Confess ~ that you are a sinner...
Romans 3:23 ~ For all have sinned and come short of the glory of God.

Romans 6:23 ~ For the wages of sin is death; but the gift
of God is eternal life through Jesus Christ our Lord.

Believe~ that God will save you from your sins...
John 3:16 ~ For God so loved the world; that He gave
His only begotten Son, that whosever, believeth in Him;
should not perish, but have everlasting life.

Acts 16:31 ~Believe on the Lord, Jesus Christ, and thou shalt be saved.

Ask ~ God to forgive you from your sins and to become the Savior
and Lord of your life...
Matthew 10:32 ~ Whosoever therefore shall confess me before
men, him will I confess also before my Father which is in heaven.

Romans 10:9 ~ That if thou shalt confess with thy mouth
the Lord Jesus, and shalt believe in thine heart that God
hath raised him from the dead, thou shalt be saved.

✝

I John 1:9 ~ If we confess our sins, he is faithful and just to forgive us our sins, and to cleanse us from all unrighteousness.

If you have confessed, believed, and asked the God of Glory to come into your heart, and be the Lord of your life, He will welcome you with open arms into His Family.

Romans 8:14-17 ~ For as many as are led by the Spirit of God, they are the sons of God. For ye have not received the spirit of bondage again to fear; but ye have received the Spirit of adoption, whereby we cry, Abba Father. The Spirit itself beareth witness with our spirit, that we are the children of God: And if children, then heirs; heirs of God, and joint-heirs with Christ;

Galatians 3:26, 27, 29 ~ For ye are all the children of God by faith in Christ Jesus. For as many of you as have been baptized into Christ have put on Christ.

And if ye be Christ's, then are ye Abraham's seed, and heirs according to the promise.

Titus 3:4-7 ~ But after that the kindness and love of God our Saviour toward man appeared, Not by works of righteousness which we have done, but according to his mercy he saved us, by the washing of regeneration, and renewing of the Holy Ghost; Which he shed on us abundantly through Jesus Christ our Saviour; That being justified by his grace, we should be made heirs according to the hope of eternal life.

Is Jesus knocking at your door? Is it your turn to answer His call? He can save you today… you just need to ask Him.

In Jesus Name. Amen.

✝

Choose you this day whom ye will serve... but as for me and my house we will serve the Lord.

~ Joshua 24:15

About the Author

My Soul Doth Magnify the Lord is the culmination of Mary ("Peggy") Wisham Fenstermacher's life work of prose and poetry. Many of her poems were written in the mid 1990's while some date back to 1988. Raised in a Christian home, Mary has participated and ministered in churches her entire life. She was afforded the privilege of attending Christian school from kindergarten through sixth grade. Mary accepted Christ as her Lord and Savior at the age of eleven, was baptized by immersion, and joined Berean Baptist Temple in her home town. Throughout her life, she has been blessed with many teachers and preachers that captivated her mind, heart, and soul with the truths in God's Word.

Now, along with these scriptures, she has written a poetry book for all people. Included is a section on the blessings of motherhood and a special children's corner where simple, childhood delights such as exploring the joy and beauty of birds, bubbles, and butterflies, will coax even the eldest reader back to the days of years gone by. Between these sections are poems on hope, faith, God's majestic creation, the blessings that come with Thanksgiving and Christmas.

Born in Bridgeton, New Jersey, Mary graduated from Bridgeton High School and attended Catawba College in Salisbury, NC, for two years. After her marriage, she continued her studies at Kutztown State University, Kutztown, PA, where she graduated magna cum laud with a B.S. Degree in Elementary Education and a concentration in English. She has taught in public and Christian schools for over 20 years and homeschooled her own children for ten years. Mary is currently the music director and organist in a local church in Dixfield, Maine, and teaches private piano lessons to area students. She lives in Peru, Maine, with her husband, Todd. They have five wonderful children, three godly sons-in law and four spunky grandchildren—all special blessings from God!

Mary has also written children's books about an adventurous, warm weather penguin that loves exploring the world around him. *Pablo Visits the Desert* (2010) and *Pablo Visits the Ocean* (2011) are the first two books of the series. They are full color books beautifully illustrated by Sandra Leinonen Dunn, artist and illustrator, also of Maine. Both books were Best Books Award Finalists in the USA Book News competition (Los Angeles, CA) for the Children's Softcover Picture Book Fiction category.

On November 16, 2012, it was announced that *Pablo Visits the Desert* was awarded Winner status in the Novelty & Gift category of the USA Book News, Best Books competition. *Pablo Visits the Ocean* was awarded Finalist status. These books were the only award recipients in this category. Book three, *Pablo Visits the Forest*, is in the making.

For information concerning Mary's publications, you may write to her address at P.O Box 39, Dixfield, Maine 04224, or e-mail her at mwfenstermacher@msn.com. Please use the title of the book in the subject line. Blessings! mwf